Behind Hospital Doors

Borderline Personality Disorder

Bad patient

Persistent attender

Despairing at prejudice

Beautiful

Person

Determined to survive

Big girl

Patient carer

Decides to move forward

A place you can be for up to two weeks
Staff support you at all hours
Some patients are sectioned, some are not
Each meal is brought on a heated trolley
Smoking happens all through the day
Sleep at night is encouraged and protected
Males and females are both here
Eating happens in the dining room
Nights it's light on or a torch in your eyes
Twelve foot walls surround the garden

Upset? Go in seclusion and scream
Noises of keys and alarms day and night
In and out the door is locked
Tuesday's meeting decides your fate

Taken there by car
Rear fence stands only six foot tall
Each patient here is female
Activities Nurse works Monday to Friday
Two floors here plus stairs and a lift
Male staff do one to ones
Each meal is cooked in the ward kitchen
Nurses work nights earlies and lates
Those with leave went to the beach

United managers and staff
No seclusion here
I am here for months not weeks
TV remote is out to use

Over the Fence

I'm the only one in the garden
I give a subtle glance
No one at the windows
This could be my chance

I push a chair to the fencing
I climb up to the top
One leg up on the splinters
A push and then a hop

I roll over. I've done it
Did anyone see me?
My feet touch ground in the car park
For these minutes I am free

I run round the back of the building
Hoping to get away
They're waiting by the car park gates
Maybe another day

They take me firmly by both arms
And march me back inside
I'm locked into the quiet room
Here there's no place to hide.

Playing Games

"I can play games too" you said
When you found me lying on my bed
With my top sleeve around my neck
And covers over my head

You threw the top on the floor
Then my bedding out of the door
Removed my bra and there was more

"Lift up now" came from your lips
You pulled my skirt down over my hips
You're a nurse not a lover
Still my stomach flips

As fast as you came you are gone
And I am left here with just one
Staff member sat staring
Staring on and on

"I can play games too" you said.

A Bad Night

Get in and stay in
I fling myself at the door
Sit there and stay there
I fight you some more

That's enough of that now
You push me to the floor
Pull my pants down and inject me
I'm going to fight some more

Father Christmas won't come
You hold me by my arms
You'll get a present from the unit
Beep beep go the alarms

Let go and leave her
You go and shut the door
I sit right up against it
I want to fight some more

What's she doing now?
I ligature right there
You come and strip my clothes off
And leave me sitting bare

There's only my mattress for cover
I dive for the darkness beneath
A man is on my constants
I hide myself underneath

Does the mattress bend and reach the floor?
The injection works I'm yawning
And I fall asleep underneath it
I'm still there in the morning

Surrounded by fences as high as the building
Eating your meals at set times of day
Care and support is there if you want it
Understanding one another comes in time
Rooms are locked from nine until four
Entertainment can be watching a nurse wash up, messily!

Help us to help you is a common refrain
Opening doors requires a staff fob
Staff wear belts with keys and pouches
People clash and compromises are found
Impulsive responses are expected yet learned from
Toilets for patients don't have seats
An alarm sounds and staff come running
Lights are on through the day and the night

Banned Items

Blue tack and chewing gum bungs up locks
Goes down staff's necks
Or stops the clocks
So
You can't have that, it's a banned item

Those knitting needles are licensed to kill
That mouth wash contains alcohol; you might drink your fill
If you can make something deadly you probably will
So
You can't have that, it's a banned item

The Time on the Clock

Let me in my room now!
No, not for another five minutes
But I want to go to my room
Room access is at four

Let me in my room
It's four o'clock already
Just open my door
No it's only five to

Just let me in my room
That clock must be slow
It's the same as the other one
So were you late for morning meeting then?

All right go to your rooms
It's four o'clock now anyway!

Why did you do it?

Why did you do it?
What were you thinking?
I don't know
Maybe because I'm stupid
And my common sense is shrinking

Why did you do it?
Where did you think you'd get?
I don't know
Maybe because I was being childish
And I haven't grown out of it yet.

Why did you do it?
How did you think we'd all feel?
I don't know
Maybe because the meds had worn off
And once more the pain was real.

Why did you do it?
You know that it wasn't fair.
I don't know
Maybe because I'm impulsive
And the open door was just there.

Why did you do it?
When we gave you so much support
I don't know
Maybe I felt I didn't deserve it
"You're too big for help" I was taught.

Why did you do it?
Out here where everybody could see?
I don't know
Maybe because I'm never alone
And I ignored everybody but me.

Why did you do it?
This certainly won't help you get out
I don't know
Maybe because I'm terrified of leaving
And who knows what that's all about

Why did you do it?
When we're all here to help you get through?
I don't know
Maybe because I think if I trust you you'll push me away
And then I don't know what I'd do.

Why did you do it?
You were fine earlier on
I don't know
Maybe because it felt as though I dropped off a cliff
And all those good feelings were gone

Why did you do it?
Why not distract yourself instead?
I don't know
Maybe because it makes me feel real and alive
Despite voices shouting "You should be dead"

Why did you do it?
Will this always be how it goes?
I don't know
Maybe because it was there, so was I
And I don't know, just because I suppose.

If only
With acknowledgements to Rudyard Kipling

If you should keep your head when all around you are losing theirs
And stay calm as she beside you shouts and swears
And greet a shouted insult with a still small voice of calm
And hand in your sharps not use them for self-harm
And greet a disaster with a muted "blinking heck"
And however bad it gets, don't tie that round your neck
And act impulsively but only from a wise mind
And self sooth when needed then you'll find
That your chance of discharge maxes
And what's more you'll get your room access!

It doesn't feel like a Thursday
For Kim

You know; it doesn't feel like a Monday
Everyone seems chilled and laid back
It's more like… a Sunday I think
Yes a Sunday

You know; it doesn't feel like a Tuesday
It should be much further through the week than that
It's more like… a Thursday I think
Yes a Thursday

You know; it doesn't feel like a Wednesday
I haven't had time for a wee all day
It's more like… a Monday I think
Yes a Monday

You know; it doesn't feel like a Thursday
All leave's been stopped because of the snow
It's more like… a Saturday I think
Yes a Saturday

You know; it doesn't feel like a Friday
There's so much I still need the doctor to do
It's more like… a Wednesday I think
Yes a Wednesday

You know; it doesn't feel like a Saturday
So many people up in the afternoon
It's more like… a Tuesday I think
Yes a Tuesday

You know; it doesn't feel like a Sunday

The bank holiday's got me all out of synch
It's more like… I don't know really
Kind of a non-day
If you know what I mean

Love across Wards

Roses are Red
Violets are Blue
I've never seen you
But I know I love you

I heard you trashed a room
I knew you were for me
But the staff put the phone down
And wouldn't let us be

They said that your business
Is not for this ward
I knew you were secluded
Their silence was hard

They say that you are vulnerable
Not sure if this is right
But I know you whisper
My name in the night

So you beat up a patient
So they'd bring you here to me
I'm more important than release
Soon they'll all see

It seems like a step back
But think what it's for
True lovers forever
On medium secure

Managers Meeting

It's my managers meeting tomorrow
It's my managers meeting tomorrow
They might let me go. They might let me out
They probably won't
But they might…

Where would I go? What would I do?
How would I carry my stuff?
They won't let me go
But they might…

It's my managers meeting today
It's my managers meeting today
They might let me go. They might let me out
They probably won't
But they might…

Does my solicitor understand what I'm trying to say?
Will they think I'm a worthless person?
They won't let me go
But they might…

It's my managers meeting right now
It's my managers meeting right now
They might let me go. They might let me out
They probably won't
But they might…

The doctor is talking round in circles
The others are supporting me just not about leaving
They won't let me go
But they might…

It was my managers meeting today
It was my managers meeting today
They might have let me go. They might have let me out

They didn't
But they might have…

At least I felt that they listened and treated me like an adult
Did I really want to leave anyway?
They didn't let me go
Next time they might…

I Miss You Puss Cat

Puss you always woke me
With your nuzzles and loud purring
Now it's "I need to look at your neck"
And somebody next door swearing

When I needed a snuggle and comfort
You were pretty much usually there
Now ten of us compete for attention
Sometimes life just isn't fair

A friend brought me one of my jumpers
And there were your hairs coarse and black
Here the end of my bed is so empty
Puss I promise you I will come back

Not Enough Staff

Can I go to the laundry?
Will you take me to my room?
Have you done that thing I asked you yet?
Can you blow up this balloon?

Can I go to the computers?
Will you let me mop the floor?
Have you found out when my visit is?
Can you let me through this door?

Can I go in the quiet room?
Will you take us for a fag?
Have you got my medication?
Can you get me a rubbish bag?

Can I go to the art room?
Will you take me for a bath?
Have you found that form I asked you for?
Can you sit and make me laugh?

NO

I just can't be in three places at once
And we haven't got enough staff!

Birthday in Hospital

Happy Birthday to You
Still in hospital; Boo!
And you've lost your room access
Happy Birthday to You

Happy Birthday to You
No seats on the loo
And the whole ward is kicking off
Happy Birthday to You

View through the Fences

It's hard to see clearly through the grill on the window
And the mesh fence and the mesh fence behind that
What is there outside this bubble?
If I got out I wouldn't know which way to run
I don't know where I am

Lots of the windows are totally blanked out with film
I peeled one off once but revealed another grill.
At night my nightmares lurk behind them.
"When did you first feel like that?" I can't remember.
I don't know where I've come from

I lose my balance if I approach the fences too fast
The two lots of mesh mess with my vision and I can't see through
People ask "Will you go back to your old life?"
I won't; that is ended
But I don't know where I'm going yet

Agitation

It's like a stinging inside me
It means I can't keep still
I try to relax and let it be
But I simply cannot chill

I pace up and down the room
What can I do? When will it end?
I'll snap or ignore a person who
I'd usually call a friend

I feel like I'm walking a tightrope
Upon a piece of thread
To stay balanced is my one hope
It snapping, me falling I dread

My hands are shuddering shaking
Tears run down my cheeks
All my insides are quaking
A minute lasts for weeks

Please just let it end now
I try to follow my breath
I must make it stop, I don't know how
Meds? Self-Harm? Death?

I can't stop the feeling inside me
I carry on pacing the room
Trying to ride it and just be
But soon it will all just go boom

Listening to an Incident

I hear you crying through the wall
It tears me in two
I hear you scream and hit your head
There's nothing I can do

There's a crash and then a splinter
I think it was a chair
You shout and scream 'Get off me'
I cry
It isn't fair

I hear your fight as they hold you
You need help but from who?
And the alarms scream on and on
I feel like kicking off too.

A Riot

Whisper, Cackle
Making us mad
Something's coming
Something bad

Rush across the room
Try and use the phone
Get stopped it's late
Wail and moan

Snuggle in the corner
Whisper cackle chaff
We try to ignore you
That really makes you laugh

We finish up our take away
They send us from the room
You throw the table after us
Crash, Bang, Boom

Alarms go off you threaten staff
With a leg torn off a chair
They lock themselves away from you
Till others can get there

You take the leg and use it
Try to smash the TV
Turns out the case is shatter proof
Win some loose some you see

The response team pin you down
They didn't bring you flowers
You haven't stopped resisting yet
Your screams go on for hours

You've totally smashed up our space
We've nowhere else to roam
I feel lost and violated
You totally trashed our home

Sweep, tinkle
Splinter, thud
Something happened
It wasn't good

Head Banging

I have to bang my head
I have to bang my head
Bang it bang it all day long
Bang it to feel right not wrong
I have to bang my head

Hit it harder there's not much time
Hit it faster they'll be coming soon
Hit it harder, hit it faster
I have to bang my head

I have to bang my head
I have to bang my head
Don't stop me yet
You've got to let
Me hit it one more time

Dive over here
They're holding me tight
Bang on the floor
Cushion in the way
I have to bang my head

I have to bang my head
I have to bang my head
Held wail fight scream
I tried to get it out before you saw me
I had to bang my head

Confusion

Am I going home?
No not yet sweetheart
I'm going home
No you need to stay with us
She's staying I'm going home
No not today, you're not well
Fuck off!

Where's my case? I need to pack.
You aren't going anywhere sweetheart
I need my case to put my clothes in
You don't need it your room is here
Get me my fucking case do I have to beg?
You aren't leaving you're not well.
Fuck off!

Don't come near me
Sweetheart open the door
Get lost! Go away!
I can't you are on observations
No I'm not
Open the door I need to see you
Fuck off!

Meditate the way to the future
Understand how your past was built
Lean on your faith like a steadfast lover
Trust when foundations seem to tilt
Instinct is the star that leads you
Forward on beyond all end
And when you ask just what to do
In peace or clamour find a friend
Talk of the beliefs of others
Hear, respect, discuss and share

Read the holy books and scriptures
Onward journeys you must dare
Over the hills and far away
Move step by step and day by day

I used to self-harm

I used to self-harm
The scars are on my arms
And when I see staples on the floor
I remember how in years before I'd have used them to self-harm
But I have too much to lose now
I used to self-harm

I used to self-harm
The scars are round my neck
And when I see a loose screw
 I think that would have been a ligature point too
When I used to self-harm
But I've too much to lose now
I used to self-harm

I used to self-harm
The scars are on my legs
And when I see a kettle or urn
I think of how once I'd have used them to burn
But I've too much to lose now
I used to self-harm

I used to self-harm
The scars are in my mind
One day I hope I'll see
The world as it is meant to be
Without thoughts of self-harm
Because I've too much to lose now
I used to self-harm

In the warm sun

The sun shines warmly
And reflects glittering
From the twenty foot fence
The pampered plants are dry in the heat
The leaves make patterns of light and shade
On the patients relaxing sleepily in the bright sun
All is peaceful
No alarm sounds
No voices are raised
No chairs bang
Birds sing
A breeze blows
And the sun shines warmly

Walking on Eggshells

It's all in a look
A tone of voice
A sharp criticism
A stammered apology
A slammed door
Someone crouching under the table

Then the explosion
Shouts screams
And the thud, thud of skull on wood
Trying to beat a way out
To crush the cage of frustration that holds us

Alarms scream
Staff run
Hands press flesh to the floor
Past and present merge

Containment
Violation
Comfort
Familiar faces melt grotesquely
Fight, fight, fight for your life
Stop your fighting end your strife
Or the needle will do it for you.

I've got post

Have you got the post yet?
I'm waiting for something
Has it been given out yet?
Is there some for me?
A letter a parcel
Even a postcard
Something to break the mundainity

Sign for the letter
Peer at the envelop
Is it handwritten or is it a bill?
Can I guess who it is from the writing
Friend or family
Jenny or Gill

Open the envelop
Skim through the contents
Somebody's written and shown that they care
I may be locked up but I'm not forgotten
And now I can boast
I got post!

Allotment Soup

Stone circle
Fire pit magic

Scaring CD's
Guard flaming marigolds
And cycling smoothies

Shake thump apples scatter
Squeak and press to amber nectar

Scattered bounty
Ruby fruit
Trees shed

Sweet tangy tickle
Titillates tongue

Sparkling synergy
With bean sentries
Standing tall

Tunnel of sound
Sooths space

Lavender wafts
From willow tabernacle
Happiness grows

Ways to make me feel flawed

Say "You're so used to struggling you can't tell that I'm on your side."

Refuse me the medication that I need to live

Then say "You have to accept that it is hard for us to understand"

Say "This is the toilet for you and this is the toilet for staff."

Say "I need your nurse to explain it without even listening to me"

Search my room and move everything

Then say "It's for your own good"

Say "Come out or we'll drag you out"

Say "You're not convincing anybody"

Say "It's not polite to ignore me" when I don't know what to say

Say "Take it or we'll hold you down and give it to you"

Say "Give it to me or do I need to strip you?"

Say "We all know Hilary's history"

Say "Just give me two minutes" then don't come back

Say "You can't leave your on a section."

Say "I have lots of important things to do I don't have time for this."

Say "We haven't enough staff to do activities

Say "Stop being difficult."

Say "Yes you can" but don't hand it over

Say "This is our Christmas don't spoil it"

Say "It'll have to go through clinical governance."

To lift me just wait, listen and tell me 'I hear what you're saying'!

Post-Traumatic Stress Disorder

Perhaps
Trust
Survives
Destruction

Waiting to Move

The strand of the future slips through my fingers
Connecting me to the abyss beyond
What will come next?
I have no answers
Only the endless pull to go on
What lies beyond the mist cloaked island of now?
There is only one was to find out
I slide along the strand
Shifting sands slip with me
Everything changes
But I'm still on an island of now
With the future slipping through my fingers

Staying on track

I wake up each morning and say
I'm going to stay on track today
I get up and wash and dress
And the shape of my body makes me calm
Anger explodes as I sit on the bed
And I feel the urge to bang my pillow
Someone downstairs is playing cupid
I remember past mistakes and think I'm human
There's glass on the pavement perhaps off a car
I pick it up then put it in my bin
I stand with the kitchen knife in my palm
And think to myself I have to self sooth
Each night I pause and say
At least I stayed on track today.

Moving on

I've been a long time waiting
For pain to pass me by
But now it's time for moving on
I'm feeling scared and shy

When I leave no one will come
Knocking on my door
I take a breath and tell myself
I don't need that anymore

I'll go and see my family
And go out with my friends
Maybe attend a festival
The fun never ends

I won't need to ask permission
To go out at night
But I still desperately want
Someone to hold me tight.

I'll go out and meet new people
Find someone of my own
And maybe one day I will have
A family of my own

Blankly Waiting

All proactivity gone

Blankness inside me

Ending my life by doing nothing

Real and unreal blurs and spins

Seeking cold floors to numb mental pain

Part of me screams to be rescued

But she seems far away

Locked out by cold blankness

Intensive Treatment Service

Intensley

Tortuous

Stories

Inside

Tornados

Still

Into

The

Silence

Interfeering

Tattlers

Stop me

Inscribe

Tall

Stones

Indecisive

Teller

Struggles with story

Ideas

Trouble

Sentries

Ice

Trembles

Stalactites

Igloos

Treat

Seals

I

Take

Solices

To my voices

You are always full of suggestions

On how to end my life

Or buy us some attention

By causing hurt and strife

I'm trying to ignore you

Or at least to drown you out

But whatever I try

Whatever I do

You're always still about

A Discussion with the inner critical parent

I hate to feel like this

You brought it on yourself

Yet another near miss

It shows your total badness

Where do we go from here?

Round again and again

Or over a drop that's shear

But there might be something better at the bottom?

Or not

Won't know unless we try

Or not....

Bad Feelings

Suffocating from within

Anger fear paranoia

Disintegrating in an internal din

Sadness frustration anger

Is she laughing at me?

Anger fear paranoia

I feel so hurt but can't let that be

Sadness frustration anger

What would it take for you to move on

Anger frustration paranoia

I feel I've tried everything and hope is gone

Sadness frustration anger

Deep in my tummy is that hard burning ball

Anger fear paranoia

Pulsing into my head chest and all

Sadness frustration anger

I'm scared that my need to be with people is bottomless

Anger fear paranoia

And there's a reason why they're busy when I'm under stress

Sadness frustration anger

Anger sadness paranoia frustration fear sadness anger

Safety Bubble

I feel like I'm locked in a bubble

It's my safety bubble

It keeps the bad things out

Mostly

But it makes the things and people outside

Distorted and scary

It keeps my scary stuff in

Where others can't reject me because of it

But it bounces around inside getting stronger and stronger

My bubble cushions my falls

But I'm scared that a big fall may pop it

I'm also scared that falling hard enough

Is the only way out of this suffocating bubble

Think on

There might be someone sleeping

When you want to scream and cry

There are others to be devastated

If you were to end it and die

Yet I feel so sad and so angry

It feels like I'm living a lie

Bottle it up bottle it up

Crush it down compact it tight

Up pressure up tension

Up inferno burn it bright

It's not fair

It's not fair that pain exists

It's not fair that everything dies

One at a time

Alone

It's not fair that you can get ill

It's not fair that others congratulate you on getting better

When you can still feel the void inside

Gaping

It's not fair when you scream and nobody comes

It's not fair that people can hurt you

So badly that it goes right through yourself

Burning

It's not fair that life's not fair

It's not fair that it begins and ends in pain

Crushing

Did I say it wrong?

I'm trying to be honest but I'm scared

That what I say may condemn me

To a life isolated and struggling

Or one imprisoned with others in my face

I'm trying to be honest but it's hard

As how I feel flips from minute to minute

And what I think is tangled with the need to punish myself

For not living up to expectations

Disappointment

But I really really wanted it!

I know but it's not going to happen

Is there something I can hit?

No! We've got to keep it all in

If they know it hurts so

They'll use it to control us

I know you wanted to go

But see what that admission brings, thus:

Don't admit to wanting anything

Tell them to go away

Stick to what you can give yourself

And shrink a little each day

I want to go home

I want to go home

Well you'll have to stop ligaturing

And take your insulin

Without any messing

I want to go home

For quiet nights that sooth and scare

And are as endless as noisy ones

Wherever I am I always want to move

I want to go home where there's

No one staring at me

Though it's empty when nobody's there

Is it worth it to be free?

Tea Cosy

What are the dimensions of your tea cosy?

Why the f***k do you want to know that?

It's ordinary sized and round

Is this your idea of a chat

What colour wool do you want?

It's for a tea cosy for Jenny

Bright or pastel? Bright please

Apart from that just any

Blue stripes green stripes red stripes too

White stripes purple stripes make something new

I keep falling asleep over my crochet

And going out like a light

Perhaps cos the wards too noisy

For me to sleep in the night

Will she like it?

Or must she grit her teeth and be polite

Still I guess the thought is there

It may not be enough but it might

Seasonal Haikus

Bare treetops

Whipped by hail

Beyond the window

Snowdrop sprouts

Beneath the bush

Sunlight streams

Air thick and heavy

Sun beats

Thunder to follow

Brown leaves crackle

Wind bites

Sun flashes through bare trees

Nurse's Hiccups

Does cinnamon give you hiccups?

I love to eat it you see

But now my gullet spasms

And its hiccup after hiccup for me

What? Any food eaten quickly?

Well I did inhale mine

Hiccups are always a risk in this job

Where we have no time to dine

I hate when you breath in and hiccup

And it sounds like a burp

Everyone turns and looks at you

 You feel like such a twerp

Hiccup hiccup hiccup

It will go on forever? It wont!

It will just feel like it

You'll have to scare me…NO DON'T!

Support Workers Apple

This apple really isn't nice

It could do with loads of spice

It's getting soft and bland as rice

My apple

There is a blemish on the side

I saw it though it tried to hide

I'm eating round it open wide

My apple

I'm only taking nibbling bites

The cores not even in my sights

I feel bad to throw it though I should by rights

My apple

I'm giving up now that is it

If I have another bite I'll have to spit

It out the base of the bin it hit

My apple

I hate community meetings

I hate community meetings

Trapped all together in a room

In some places they are compulsory

10 minutes late is your doom

There always seem to be arguments

It's still personal with no names

Or it's "staff do it too" and between me and you

Opens a chasm that shames

I don't like community meetings

It's a time to announce new rules

And put us in our place down there in disgrace

And generally make us feel fools

I don't like community meetings

When pressure gets turned on the staff

And they feel like a target is pinned to their heads

And it's no longer possible to laugh

MDT

I've sometimes run from MDT

And truths I don't want to face

Or withdrawn inside to make things be

As though I was not in that place

It feels like a place of judgement

Are things better worse or the same

Same I think is how things went

But if they think worse I'm to blame

I'm scared of asking for things

Just in case they say no

And I fall apart and my stress bell dings

Or conditions set mean I can't go

There's so many eyes in the room,

Looking in my direction

I feel a sense of impending doom

The joys of being on a section!

Multi-Disciplinary Team

Model employees

Defend

Trust

Moaning

Dictators

Twittering

Morning

Drags

Terribly

Medicating

Draconians

Talk

Mardy

Doctor

Terrorises

Many

Decisions

Talked about

Moreish

Date slices

Teapots

Monotonous

Droning

Terminates

My sock

My sock is short and pink

To look at it you wouldn't think

It could be a weapon

Around my neck it stretched tight

Making my insides feel right

It's a life saver

I'm worried someone will challenge me

But I'm getting away with it how can this be

It's invisible

I take it off and it's in my hand

My insides squiggle like shifting sand

It's an invitation

I give in and put it back

My nerves abruptly cease to rack

It's PRN

I take it off and analyse the chain

A mixture of opportunity, impulse, pain

It's an icebreaker

Broad mind

Enthusiasm

Altruism

Understanding

Tenacity

Insightful

Feelings

Unbowed

Laughter

Working

Orderliness

Mischief

Assertiveness

Nurturing

Losing it

You have to take control now

Come on calm down

I can't it's still boiling inside me

I have to self-harm

You've self-harmed already

Have you seen your head

Of course I haven't

My eyes are in my face!

I have to do more yet

Let go of me

Let go of me

Let me bang my head

Challenging Voices

I will do whatever I like all right!

Walk to the shops and feel the breeze

Without all your attempts to tease

Sit quietly on my bed

Without you screaming in my head

Talk to my family and my friends

You interrupt the conversation ends

Take my medication without fear

With your comments nothings clear

Sooth myself in a nice hot bath

Without how you cruelly point and laugh

Get out of here and live my life

However much you cause me strife

I will do whatever I like all right!

Self-Harm

I need to self-harm

I'll tie a sock around my neck

You've wrenched it from my grasp

There must be another way

I have to self-harm

I'll smash my head upon the wall

You pin me then march me down the hall

There must be another way

I have to self-harm

I worm my way off the mat

You drag me back and that is that

There must be another way

Lorazapam, Lavender, talking, crying

Being held, comfort, screaming sighing

All of them helped me through

But they seemed locked away

Until after I self-harmed

Nurse's Handmade skirt

It's like just the coolest thing ever

Just you wait till you see

I've even sewn a zip in the back

And nobody has one but me

It's covered in cartoon strips

I may have made some mistakes

But never the less I made it

I've really got what it takes

I bought a book on dressmaking

And found out what could go wrong

I'm going to make me a dress next

I'm sure it won't take me long

Hearing about the Nurses dog

Whacker Dog!

Toaster is scary

Bearded Dog

Fluffy and hairy

Feet on the window ledge

Bark at the swans

Ducks on the garden

Door opens he's gone

Chase down the garden

Splash and a splat

In the canal

Out like a drowned rat

Trim up his eyebrows

Hover his beard

He loves to get his face sucked

It's really weird

Bearded dog

Fluffy and hairy

Whacker dog

Toaster is scary

Ready to try new solutions

Endlessly picking yourself up

Caring about what happens

Ordinarily living in the present

Variable some days you dip

Encouraging yourself and others

Real life is your adventure

Yes it's the time to begin

Consultant's New Glasses

I used to be just long sighted

But I'm short as well now

I'm sure I will get used to it

But sometimes I wonder how!

In my new glasses the world jumps out at me

Instead of a comforting fuzz

I'll try and reach the office without hitting anything

I don't want to make a fuss

Full of promise and of fear

Until you feel the end is near

Treasures around to be dug up

Unsure of how full the cup

Ready for anything till it happens

Expect the unexpected see through the lens

Peopled with ghosts

Another time another place

Sleeping lions may wake and pounce

Tale care if you travel here

Pinpoint balance between past and future

Rushes past minute by minute

Easy to miss if not mindful

Sensation is here

Eventful NS REAL

Never returns

Trust yourself to live in it

Let me go home!

I want to go home NOW!

Hindsight says the answer is no

This package couldn't support you

And back into hospital you would go

Then you would be there a long time

Because your confidence had been knocked

That's already happened when you left in the summer

The effect on you has been clocked

Is it like removing a band-aid?

Rushing through the steps so fast

We're going to get comfy with each one

For a different outcome to the past

I'm sorry

I'm sorry so sorry

I never made it as an adult

I don't have a job or pay my way

I can't spell properly

I don't keep the house tidy

I don't drive

I haven't a partner

I have no children

Half the time I'm scared of my own shadow

I really am sorry

Can you love me anyway?

And finally....

Speak

You will be heard

Listen

To the small positive voice inside

Shout

When you are angry

Cry

When you are sad

Run

And chase rainbows

Dream

Fantastic dreams

And remember…

You have positive people rooting for you

And they are always on your side

www.ingramcontent.com/pod-product-compliance
Lightning Source LLC
Chambersburg PA
CBHW070301290526
45791CB00003B/1040